FOOD BRANDS WE LOVE

M&M MARS

By Kaitlyn Duling

Kaleidoscope
Minneapolis, MN

The Quest for Discovery Never Ends

This edition is co-published by agreement between Kaleidoscope and World Book, Inc.

Kaleidoscope Publishing, Inc.
6012 Blue Circle Drive
Minnetonka, MN 55343 U.S.A.

World Book, Inc.
180 North LaSalle St., Suite 900
Chicago IL 60601 U.S.A.

Kaleidoscope ISBNs
978-1-64519-213-8 (library bound)
978-1-64519-281-7 (ebook)

World Book ISBN
978-0-7166-4191-9 (library bound)

Library of Congress Control Number
2020936273

Developed and produced by Focus Strategic Communications Inc.

Printed in the United States of America.

Bigfoot lurks within one of the images in this book. It's up to you to find him!

TABLE OF CONTENTS

Chapter 1

Melts in Your Mouth

Joy ripped open a corner of the small, brown bag. Tiny, round candies spilled out. She saw a rainbow of colors: red, orange, green, blue, yellow, and brown. The candies clinked into the bowl.

M&M's come in six colors.

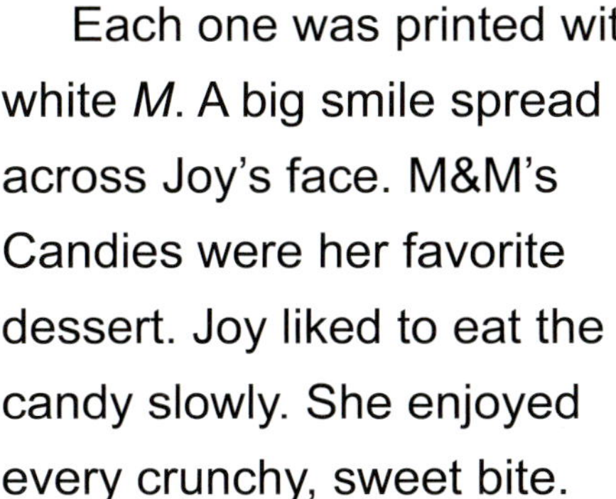

Each one was printed with a white *M*. A big smile spread across Joy's face. M&M's Candies were her favorite dessert. Joy liked to eat the candy slowly. She enjoyed every crunchy, sweet bite.

FUN FACT

The Ms in M&M's stand for Mars and Murrie. Those are the last names of the two partners who created the candy—Forrest Mars and Bruce Murrie.

Lots of people eat M&M's in order of their colors.

Joy lined up the blue M&M's in her palm and ate them one by one. She thought of the popular M&M's slogan. "Melts in your mouth, not in your hand," had been used since the 1960s. That was more than 60 years ago.

The Columbia *took its first flight on April 21, 1981.*

M&M's have been around for decades. Joy's mom and grandma both ate them as kids. They even remembered when M&M's went into space. It was way back in 1981. NASA put M&M's on the *Columbia* space shuttle. They were the first candies in space.

FUN FACT

More than 400 million M&M's are produced each day. About 50 percent are made in a factory in New Jersey.

M&M's have their own little candy mascots.

Joy is not alone in her love for M&M's. Over the years, M&M's have become an American icon. They have a rich history and memorable **advertisements**. The M&M's spokescandies have starred in countless ads. Today, M&M's are one of the most popular candies in the United States. Of course, their sweet taste does not hurt.

M&M's are owned by a company called Mars, Incorporated. The $37 billion company is one of the largest food companies in the world. Mars employs 125,000 people in more than 80 countries. Mars makes other candies, such as Snickers and Skittles. M&M's have been made by Mars since the very beginning. They do not plan to stop anytime soon.

The Snickers slogan is, "You're not you when you're hungry!"

Chapter 2
History of M&M's

To understand M&M's, you have to travel back in time to 1932. That is when Forrest Mars got into a big fight with his father. His dad managed the Mars candy company. Forrest was so angry, he moved to England. There, he made Mars bars for soldiers. During the Spanish Civil War of the late 1930s, Forrest noticed something. He saw British soldiers eating miniature chocolate candies. Each candy had a hard sugar shell. The shell kept the candies from melting.

Forrest Mars soon returned to the United States. He kept thinking about those candies. Forrest went to Bruce Murrie, son of Hershey **executive** William Murrie. He told Bruce about his idea. The two decided to go into business together.

FUN FACT

The *M* stamp was first added to M&M's in 1950. The first stamps were black. The white *M* used today was introduced in 1954.

The Pall Mall in London, England, circa 1930.

Just like they do today, Mars placed ads in magazines for their candies during the 1940s.

In 1941, Forrest and Bruce began to **manufacture** M&M's. The candies were originally sold in cardboard tubes. The packages looked a bit like toilet paper tubes. The original candy colors were brown, red, orange, yellow, green, and violet.

During World War II, M&M's were not sold in stores. They were provided to the military. The chocolate did not melt, so it was easy to send overseas. Soldiers got hooked on the candy. After the war, they kept eating more and more M&M's.

American troops during World War II.

After World War II, M&M's popularity grew. They added new flavors and fillings. They changed the colors and the packaging. Mars continued to create new candies, too. In the 1960s, the company launched M&M's Fruit Chews. The short-lived candy would later become Starburst. But M&M's has continued to be Mars' number one **brand**.

A SWEET RIVALRY

Today, Hershey and Mars are rivals. They compete for the same customers. However, when M&M's were first created, Hershey supplied the chocolate for M&M's. After a few years, the companies went their separate ways.

MARS BRAND TIMELINE

1941
M&M's Plain Chocolate Candies first come out.

1945
M&M's Peanut Chocolate Candies make their first appearance.

1948
The M&M's brown pouch package makes its debut.

1950
The *M* appears on the candies for the first time.

1954
The tagline "Melts in Your Mouth, Not in Your Hands" comes out.

1976
Orange joins the mix of colors, replacing red.

1982
M&M's become the first candies in space.

1984
M&M's become the official snack food of the Olympic Games.

1986
Red M&M's return.

1941 1945 1948 1950 1954 1976 1982 1986

1989
M&M's Peanut Butter Chocolate Candies make their debut.

1990
M&M's become a sponsor of NASCAR.

1995
Blue M&M's replace the tan-colored M&M's.

1997
The M&M's WORLD store opens in Las Vegas, Nevada.

2000
M&M's become the official candies of the new millennium.

2004
My M&M's launches and customers can design their own M&M's.

2008
The FACES project allows customers to add pictures to their M&M's.

2010
M&M's Pretzel Candies come out.

2012
A new spokescandy, Ms. Brown, debuts during the Super Bowl.

2017
M&M's arrive in India.

1989 1990 1995 2000 2004 2008 2012 2017

Chapter 3

Making My M&M's

It is a sunny morning in Hackettstown, New Jersey. Lara is arriving at the M&M's factory. As she heads inside, she can already smell the chocolate.

Lara wears a white lab coat. She pulls on gloves and safety glasses. A hair net, ear plugs, and hard hat complete the look. After washing her hands, Lara is ready to make some M&M's.

FUN FACT

In 2000, M&M's were named the candies of the new millennium. The Roman numeral M stands for "1000." The candies' name adds up to 2000.

Mars' North American candy factory is in New Jersey.

MARS
chocolate
north america

Lara's factory is home to M&M's, Peanut M&M's, and **custom** products. Since 2004, customers have been able to design their own M&M's. On the My M&M's website, there are M&M's in different colors, such as black and gold.

M&M's have different color themed candies for holidays like Valentine's Day, Christmas, and Halloween.

There are M&M's printed with emojis and photos. There are even M&M's with messages such as, "Will you marry me?" Customers buy custom M&M's for gifts and holidays. Some buy them just for fun. Just like classic M&M's, the custom products start with chocolate.

FUN FACT

In 1995, Mars decided to replace the tan M&M's. The company held a contest. Fans could vote for their favorite color. The options were blue, pink, and purple. About 10 million people voted. Blue won with 54 percent of the vote.

M&M's stores feature walls of multi-colored candies.

Lara walks by the large vats of chocolate. There, the **ingredients** are mixed together. The chocolate is heated very carefully. Then, it is made into small circles. The circles are sent through a cooling tunnel. At the end, the M&M's are given their colorful coatings. Lara helps make millions of M&M's every day. The job is pretty sweet.

A ROCK 'N ROLL RULE

In the 1980s, the rock band Van Halen was often on tour. At concerts, the band members always requested M&M's to eat in the dressing room. But there was one important detail: there could be no brown M&M's. Fans thought the band was being too picky. But Van Halen later said that the request ensured the concert planners were paying close attention to the contract.

Chapter 4
What's Your Favorite Flavor?

Hank looked around the store. It was covered in the M&M's **logo**. There were M&M's toys and M&M's posters. There were even M&M's pillows on the shelves. Hank loved anything with M&M's on it. He was a **fanatic**.

M&M's were Hank's favorite candies. He loved them so much, he wanted to try every flavor. Over the years, Mars had released plenty of options. There were M&M's filled with peanut butter and caramel. Some crunched with almonds or pretzels. There was even a dark chocolate flavor. In the fall, Hank had tried a white chocolate pumpkin pie flavor. He was not too sure about that one.

The M&M's World store in Shanghai, China has two floors.

Almost any product with M&M's logos or characters can be found in the store.

M&M's stores are colorful and impressive all around the world.

Hank is not the only one who loves M&M's. Mars' best-selling candy is popular around the world. M&M's are sold in more than 100 countries. In addition to the bite-sized candies, the brand now sells candy bars.

Each chocolate bar is filled with M&M's. M&M's even come in different sizes. M&M's Mega are an extra-large version. You can buy teeny-tiny M&M's Minis. They are sold in plastic tubes. They look similar to the brand's original cardboard tube.

FUN FACT

In 2017, M&M's was the top-ranked candy brand in the United States. The brand had about $688 million in yearly sales. That is nearly two times the amount made by Hershey, the number two brand in the country.

M&M's release special colors and mixes for movies as well.

There are so many different types of M&M's to choose from.

It has been about 80 years since M&M's were first created. Since then, the package has changed. There have been tweaks to the flavor lineup. New colors have also been added. Despite the changes, M&M's are still an important part of the Mars family. For many fans, the candies are a big part of their lives, too.

M&M'S GO GLOBAL

In 2019, Mars introduced three new Peanut M&M's flavors in the United States. Each was inspired by a different country. Coconut Peanut was inspired by Thailand. Jalapeño Peanut had Mexican flavors. English Toffee Peanut rounded out the trio. It was inspired by the United Kingdom. The candies were not a huge hit.

Blue is cool. Red is classic and smart. Yellow is friendly and happy. Brown is intelligent. Green is confident. Orange is always scared.

BEYOND THE BOOK

After reading the book, it's time to think about what you learned. Try the following exercises to jumpstart your ideas.

THINK

THAT'S NEWS TO ME. M&M's have a long, rich history. Consider how you learn about foods and brands. What information can be found in news articles? What about news programs on TV? Where can you go to find news you can trust?

CREATE

PRIMARY SOURCES. Primary sources provide firsthand accounts of an event. Interviews, videos, and photographs are all examples of primary sources. Create a list of the kinds of primary sources you might be able to find about M&M's.

DISCOVER

WHAT'S YOUR OPINION? The text states that M&M's is Mars' number one brand. Do you agree with that statement? Provide evidence from the text to support your opinion. Share your position and evidence with a friend. Does your friend find the argument convincing?

GROW

DRAWING CONNECTIONS. Create a diagram that shows and explains the connections between Mars and Hershey. How does learning about the history of these companies help you better understand candy brands?

Visit www.ninjaresearcher.com/2138 to learn how to take your research skills and book report writing to the next level!

SEARCH LIKE A PRO
Learn how to use search engines to find useful websites.

FACT OR FAKE?
Discover how you can tell a trusted website from an untrustworthy resource.

TEXT DETECTIVE
Explore how to zero in on the information you need most.

SHOW YOUR WORK
Research responsibly—learn how to cite sources.

WRITE

GET TO THE POINT
Learn how to express your main ideas.

PLAN OF ATTACK
Learn prewriting exercises and create an outline.

Further Resources

BOOKS

Bullis, Amber. *Mindfulness and Food*. Minneapolis, MN: Jump!, 2020.

Green, Sara. *Hershey's*. Hopkins, MN: Bellwether Media, 2015.

Owings, Lisa. *Tasting*. Hopkins, MN: Bellwether Media, 2018.

Schuh, Mari. *Dentists*. Hopkins, MN: Bellwether Media, 2018.

WEBSITES

FACTSURFER

Factsurfer.com gives you a safe, fun way to find more information.

1. Go to www.factsurfer.com.
2. Enter "M&M Mars" into the search box and click 🔍
3. Select your book cover to see a list of related websites.

Glossary

advertisements: Notices or announcements for products or services to persuade people to buy them.

brand: The name of a product made by a company.

custom: Something made or designed for a particular customer.

executive: Someone who is a senior manager in a business organization.

fanatic: A person who is devoted to something beyond normal limits.

ingredients: Components that are combined to make a food or product.

logo: A unique symbol or design mark that identifies a product.

manufacture: To make something from raw materials, usually in large quantities, using machinery.

millennium: A period of a 1,000 years or the anniversary of the passage of that time.

Index

PHOTO CREDITS

The images in this book are reproduced through the courtesy of: emka74/Shutterstock Images, front cover (Mars bar); Abramova Elena/Shutterstock Images, front cover (Twix bar), p. 13 (Mars bar); bestv/Shutterstock Images, front cover (Skittles); Sergiy Kuzmin/Shutterstock Images, front cover (candy coated chocolates), pp. 1, 7, 31; Roman Samokhin/Shutterstock Images, front cover (M&M's), pp. 13 (M&M's packages), 14 (top right); foxaon1987/Shutterstock Images, p. 1 (background); BORIMAT PRAOKAEW/Shutterstock Images, pp. 3, 27 (bottom); Emilio100/Shutterstock Images, pp. 4-5 (M&M's package), 14 (bottom left); Evan-Amos/Public Domain, pp. 4-5 (M&M's); Nano Calvo/Alamy Stock Photo, p. 6; NASA, p. 7 (top); Home Bird/Alamy Stock Photo, p. 8; Mehaniq/Shutterstock Images, p. 9; Ekaterina_Minaeva/Shutterstock Images, pp. 10, 14 (bottom right); Lionel Green/Archive Photos/Getty Images, p. 11 (top); Jeff Morgan 09/Alamy Stock Photo, p. 11 (bottom); Everett Collection/Shutterstock Images, p. 12; Sheila Fitzgerald/Shutterstock Images, p. 13 (Hershey bar); David Adam Kess/CC BY-SA 4.0, pp. 14 (top left), 19; Urbano Delvalle/The LIFE Images Collection/Getty Images, p. 15 (top); Chris McGrath/Getty Images, p. 15 (bottom left); Felix Choo/Alamy Stock Photo, pp. 15 (bottom right), 22; Oleksandr Kostiuchenko/Shutterstock Images, p. 16; Frank Paul/Alamy Stock Photo, pp. 16-17; Kristoffer Tripplaar/Alamy Stock Photo, pp. 18-19; Anton_Ivanov/Shutterstock Images, pp. 20-21; Fryderyk Gabowicz/picture-alliance/dpa/AP Images, p. 21; Paul McKinnon/Shutterstock Images, p. 23 (top); Tooykrub/Shutterstock Images, p. 23 (bottom); Christian Mueller/Shutterstock Images, p. 24; Keith Homan/Shutterstock Images, p. 24 (M&M's chocolate bar); khaffizzul hakim/Shutterstock Images, p. 25 (top); SophieOst/Shutterstock Images, p. 25 (bottom); Stephen Chernin/Getty Images, p. 26; dcwcreations/Shutterstock Images, p. 27 (top).

About the Author

Kaitlyn Duling's favorite M&M's color is blue. She has written more than 100 books for children. She lives in Washington, D.C.